SONATA in B MINOR

Edited, with realization of
the basso continuo, by
RICHARD PLATT

JOHN RANISH
(1693 - 1777)

I

II

4

SONATA in B MINOR

I

FLUTE
Edited, with realization of
the basso continuo, by
RICHARD PLATT

JOHN RANISH
(1693 - 1777)

Printed in Great Britain

OXFORD UNIVERSITY PRESS MUSIC DEPARTMENT, GREAT CLARENDON STREET, OXFORD OX2 6DP

II

Allegro

III

OXFORD UNIVERSITY PRESS

SONATA in B MINOR

VIOLONCELLO

Edited, with realization of
the basso continuo, by
RICHARD PLATT

I

JOHN RANISH
(1693 - 1777)

II

Allegro

III

Giga

III

Giga